Praise for *Trash Witch*

Always smart and filled with a laconic wit and an intricate layer of mystery, Martha McCollough's poems in her newest collection *Trash Witch* offer expertly elliptical phrasings that soar and quiver with a Patti Smith-like swerve, then jam with the universe and our dystopian world with a wild, one-of-a-kind, born-of-ashes strength and virtuosity. This is a book that shows what poetry can do—pausing to listen to the stars and observe all that is beautiful in the universe, conversing with ghosts, rats, crows, and the fathomless desecrated earth, hungering for more, and delighting in the found. "I console myself / with a handful of bright seeds / not for hunger / but their red translucent gleam." These are deeply compassionate and articulate poems, powered by love, by one of our finest poets.

—Suzanne Mercury, author of *Hive*

You'll want to read these poems twice. As in her previous book, *Wolf Hat Iron Shoes,* the links between the seemingly sparse phrases light up enriching "ah-ha" moments. McCollough is no absentee stylist. She inhabits these lines, as in the title poem: "her dream hut / spins in the thicket / on chicken-bone legs…"

—Richard Wayne Horton, author of *Artists in the Underworld*

Trash Witch

MARTHA McCOLLOUGH

LILY POETRY REVIEW BOOKS

Underneath all reason lies delirium, drift.
—Gilles Deleuze

I don't care I love it.
—Icona pop

Contents

Trash Witch

As far as this world goes

everything almost   not here

     a bubble

        burst to mist

still I get out of bed   go to work   for decades

        though it has come to my attention that I will die

     I should have tunneled out   I had my spoon

      the days slipped by

         just keeping the atoms organized

        patted into the shape

        of a body

      until   undone by some bungle

the structure gives way   like a balsa wood bridge

      tested to failure

        reverting to prior condition

      as pile of sticks

Picnic on the moon

rabbit   woodcutter   princess
cups of pale tea   peeled eggs
    on blank porcelain

half finished sentences
   cut off by sleep—

immortal patrons of lunacy
   sharp shadowed
    watching all night

below, a dog with an air
   of menace leads me
     along the black canal

Cold crows

pine bending
downwind
roar and sigh

sumac lace
sum of lack
and lakeside

horses still strange
in their fly masks

cracking under heel
sky birdless
dusk the correct hour
flickers awake

high tangled
bittersweet
airy early ice
a black window

Trash witch

1.
sneaking the woods
by lastlight to sift all
you don't want—hope
you burnt the shreds
of your haircut—
in her kitchen a little doll
wrapped in a scrap
of your suit

her tattoo in hieroglyphs
she poked with a sewing needle
should have been stitching
a rose on a pillowcase

to think they thought
they could make her
sit up straight

2.
her dream hut
spins in the thicket
on chicken-bone legs
a rusty two-tone truck

bigger inside than out
the better to house
layers of drugstore scifi
old nests   bent orreries
all her trifles

lucky stub
ashed on a plate
black fakenails
scratching
redlined arms
crumbs on velvet
she says what card
am I holding

3.
why has no one offered her
a suitcase full of money
some compensation
for being alive

4.
a cold desert   harsh and salty
how is it here   head of a dog
poking from the ditch it says
take me in   my eyes: infinity sad
she says   *my familiar*

shouldn't asmodea sweep her up
pink cape flowing over the hills
as soldiers hunt the burnt fields

one eye a blur
the other a green
landscape

5.
her mournful planet—
something digging
out from the ashes
trying to get born

into her thicket
gather all the birds

she's carried off
yelling   *uhoh myth*

it's a chilly honor
to be pinned
among the stars

her crown's a rake's end
a glittering fence
adorned with tears

her consolation
is her uselessness

When to wear a tiara

above a black cotton mask
while assembling a model guillotine
          with prehistoric tigerskin coat
     amethyst chunks wired into a glittering landslide
looking for a child among the lost
      a lattice of eyes
                    in the ashes of the house
            while rowing over a drowned city

La merveilleuse

A thin red ribbon around the neck
      like a guillotined aristo   reassembled
exquisite in ragged lace
           & prison haircut
   dressed for the *bal des victimes*
         flirting a broken fan
             all flinching all the time

Bookish house

beneath the floorboards
even the rat's composing its memoirs
on the backs of my ancient homework

(blotty blue cursive
list of kinds of coal—
anthracite bituminous lignite—
a diagrammed sentence
chief exports of south america

nun's red penciled blah blah blah)
my childish diligence

no one cares about any of that
thinks the rat, correctly

Invisible friends

mine were always animals
as there were enough
people in the house already

my guardian angel
wasn't exactly a friend

I'd seen its picture
its worried expression
in my Catholic coloring book

looming sad sergeant
of rules I meant to evade

I dreamed of being an animal
hidden, taskless

of sneaking down
to the lake at night
slipping in smooth as a tooth

let's go whispered my little blue dog
my affectionate lion
my bad monkey

The Minotaur is named Asterion

—after an etching by Picasso

Ariadne or Marie Therese
lifts her useless candle

tossing his bull-heavy head
Asterion follows—once
he thought she might rescue *him*

at his feet lie a furious dying horse
a broken matador with the face
of Marie Therese

Asterion stamps the stones
he wishes his sword were a thread
he could follow back into the dark

at far left by ladder Christ escapes
toward heaven or his cross

behind all that the sea
lit by one scudding sail—
            who is coming

Night Comes

frogs like bells

      hum of starlight

           hour of unknown birds

  when no man can work

 clicks and creaks

       a dark house falling asleep

            engaged in night's lawful occupation

discordant breath of a mile-away train

soft voice telling a story—

      purposely dull

         then a shrieky party weaving through the trees

   coyotes' traveling festivities

     say villain's the way to go

Moon

the moon smells like a burnt curl of caps   a dry garden

tilled by tiny blows   the grey gunpowder moon frowns

lonely for the ocean   your cells   your half-full glass

the full moon hangs beside a streetlight—look, twins!

crescent, she rocks on her back   a boat in the daylit sky

Land's end

So many birds used to be girls, so many flowers,
there's hardly a natural creature out here in the fields.
When the wind picks up, any weed might speak to
you of pursuit and desperation. All the trees in the
forest are Daphne's grandchildren. The moon is full:
she's keeping an eye on her girls. Sometimes a really
sad one dissolves into the sea.

Pale queen of this trailer park

this winter everyone has fled
   packing up the airstreams
to head for the warm south

clouds billow from the gorges
bare trees bathe in a cold haze

In our rusty palace
    forgot effort
    forgot light
      though I was sick for light

I lounged on creaking Naugahyde
      his black throne
        of bad moods
next to a grim god
      whom nothing could amuse
    Spring abandoned me
        and so, like everything, I was
        a disappointment

I had to remind him:
after all *he* stole *me*

say I have a weakness for difficult men
    if it makes you feel better

say it's only a season

will winter never end?
not here,
    parked in his withered garden
    while his snarling dog patrols
      the invisible fence

even so sometimes I sneak away
    into the still forest
        to meet with deer

    to see an ermine poke
        up through snow:

I console my cold self
    with a handful of bright seeds
        not for hunger
      but their red translucent gleam

Sharp dressed man

callcrow king
mobbed under
wings blueblacker
than top hats
all those little
gentlemen
on the strut
in the straw
white eyes gleam
feathering
the nesty beard
come running   bring
him a ring   a stickpin
stab it in   clean
as you can
glittering links
held together
with black ties
with trinkets
and formality
crow crazy

Condors

I saw one caged alone in Salt Lake City:
 all mournful stillness

the shock when it stirred, raising
huge wings like a threat of storm

a plumy hanging judge
head a bony pink fist

wild condors sleep prone, heads
tucked, in mountain treetops

under expressionist moonlight
harsh and hard-edged

each day the stately arrival at the deathbed
the grisly funeral rites and chattering wake

soaring, the condor forgets it is tagged, measured
unaware that it transmits a signal

knows the one thing: everyone
living wants to keep on and cannot

August Natterer, his visions

accompanied   or pursued across the page   by an inky crocodile
here is the witch   who made the world   in her antique hat
too homely for the job   more the small-time type   to lure lost children
to her edible forest hut   smelling of cake & bones   from the folds of her skirt
coded messages flutter   for him   sinner & secret emperor   his visions begin
with a white dot   in a white cloud   spinning rapidly   shepherd   serpent
horn pouring out light   a face made of meadow and moonlakeleaf
the other (graveyard) face of the witch   all tombstone teeth
he has painted *My eyes at the moment of the apparition*
scorched scarlet

That clock silent for years

I still mean to play ghost music
on the legless toy piano.

A pot of mercurial silver
catches moonlight.

A stone pillow, cat-shaped, I shelved
high with books I won't read again.

Silhouette horn, I waited with you
for silent tristero's empire.

What *about* apollo and dionysos
and the sadness of things, the difficult

people I loved for being difficult,
puzzles with a missing final piece.

Difficulty

call it a slammed door
a monotone hallway

eye parched
by implacable rhythms
page: a thorny orchard

we are just secret
velvet draped over
knobby scaffolds

heart: a flattened
supermarket rose

Day

the day is a casual reader
misinterpreting the light

on the table
grasses of forgetfulness

the book half under
the bed is wide awake
& preaching to the cats

July

The birds all silent. A red insect lands on my arm
and bites, just where they drew blood yesterday. The
feverfew that came in the mail is almost dead—
still there is one green stem. The day is too hot for
planting but I plant it anyway. That is called hope.
On the table tiny black ants swarm an empty cup.
I whisper *you can come back from this*

Night sky

all night earth faces
outward turning
       its back on the fire

it's not wrong
to feel uneasy
       looking up

       beyond the flat map
           of constellations

so much indifference
       outside this bubble
       of breath

* * *

or look into the forest—
     hierarchy or circle
     of dread

tigers afraid
     of elephants afraid
         of bees

     we live
       somehow
       among the fierce bees

* * *

light hides
  so much

each morning offers
a new amnesty   excuses
                the merciless world

after uncanny hours
        homesick
        for who knows what

we are
 in spite of
        everything

Behind you

light doesn't tire
to fall in a weary arc

& rattle like lost keys
on the floor of space

it just goes
straight on

then
it bangs
into something

light you
came so far
to be swallowed
by my black dress

stitched to invisibility

behind you
the starless past

Imago

what if I wake up
changing

      vanished caterpillar
       thin wings & thready limbs

present already but what if
the hour doesn't arrive or what if

      the veil, lifted, reveals
      another veil

All that is solid

hard nut of being
rough as shagbark

the work of standing up
(and they call gravity weak)

all this earthiness
a veil over nothing

then where did these
bruises come from

* * *

face up on the picnic table
counting stars

I have no idea how to live—
let's just be ghosts

Restlessness

Hummingbirds thrum like toy planes. The strawberry
plants throw out a few pink flowers—too little, too late.
I have pulled clover and chickweed, snapped the brittle
lily stems. At evening a bear crosses the backyard. The
lives of animals must be like a dream: this happens,
then this, then this. Then time to go.

The suffering of suffering

I don't have to be anywhere
or speak, though I might—

in this one way
it's good to be old

transient bubble of peace
before the suffering sets in

years rolling downhill
abyss a step away

a child steps along the curb
arms out, wavering

as if on a tightrope
as if a long fall were visible

enjoying imaginary risk—
in the distance war

washes back and forth
over the world

Dreamlike

When I say "like a dream" I mean:
you walk down a forest path
the forest pinches and narrows
    until you balance on
        the last fallen
           sapling

    I can't explain
    the tendency to exist
    things arise, okay

leaf litter
cartoonish mushrooms
    low languid clouds
        slouching over hilltops

a series of words I juxtapose
    might not be a thought
        still a thought   might
        assemble itself

music stumbles over
a flood of vocabulary

skips branch to branch
    seeking a point of entry

oh idle days

world careening
      toward silence and cold

in the meantime (meantime I love)
night's insects grow loud, exuberant

      let's go somewhere dark
      and look at the stars

The weaver

into the forest's blue eye
a rush of swan brothers

burst on a day of labor:
shirt shirt shirt and so on

order drawn
from a nest of nettles

elderberry whistle
minor glimmering

from grey thicket
a skulking prince

or predator's
interested stare

Nocturne

green september
of rain and rain

ant kingdoms
flooded

geraniums
drowned in their pots

the sky starless
the moon a blur

I turn my pillow
for the hundredth time

when will oblivion
well up like water

I don't want to dream
or remember dreams

of all the sins
my favorite is sloth

Thunder on the mountain

aspens' sharp spark
against black brushstrokes
against gray sky
mountains draped
in watery blur

it is well to remain below

the lake is still
the brook rushes into it   out of it
yellow willow twigs   deep of pines piling
up the mountain's side
toward the cold zone of *no*

small things can be accomplished

half-finished silvery light
thunder from a distance
trail rivered with rain
a hummingbird works the brook's edge—
rain sends him home

Disputed territories

the night massive   light-winged

        a vacancy   carried on the air

lantern
little device
of beauty

behind a wall pocked with shell holes

       the cards keep my creepy secrets—

minor romance
with death   desire's
embarrassments—

between a pack of cards

         and pack of wolves

I choose wolves-at-a-distance
 howling to a ruined piano
 as the tanks approach

pinwheel of sparks

      the velocity   and the sensation

Cosmographia particularis

sun   a frilled lizard   a burning glass
          warming bees into hum

moon   lost tooth
          key from a toy piano
          ivory sweetsour   plink

winter   empire of paper ghosts
          a medicine for empty

time   dream glazed   recessive

being   notice the desperate confusion

desire   simple action figure   mint in box

dirt   the graceless edge
          old animal   gasp and collapse

ocean   swimmers   clouding the deep eye

window   little blue book of starlight
          sleeve of tears

Gnossienne No. 1

tell me
ghost hand
strolling the keyboard

a way out
of the underworld

tiptoe
furtive
in the faraway

or at hand
insouciant

a scribbled
flight path

damselflies
all casual
against the air

Gnossienne No.2

between shops
a mountain
leans in

nothing made
looks right

ramshackle
gasping

the body's
bird heart
thrums

breath
intimate with sky

under circles
of stony judges

aspen exhaling
sharp green

oh altitude

Gnossienne No. 3

clouds like gray birds,
soft, hostile

rain taps the metal table
the strawberry leaves

flickering
all forlorn

untranslatable
grace notes

something offered
to the merciless world

planets roll uncalled
above the visible

flipped coins
to determine nothing

outcome:
a page in ribbons

Solstice

Through tree silhouettes all night
   mournful angels rustle
   among the ink-dark pines
a cloud blurs the moon
    pallid signal blinking
      off   on   off
at last
a breathing creature
   antlers struck brief gold
      tips the balance
        by wishing

all that wants to be
all that is exhausted
invert in stately motion

  a vast capsize—

behind all order
  or appearance of order
    chaos mutters and coughs

reason: your flimsy hut
  in the delirious forest
one candle flickering all the long night
   around it   patter and hush
   rain on the leaves or furtive parade
         of monsters
in the distance   music, gunfire, car crash
  under your feet roots
     go about
     their fractal busyness
    overhead the canopy   leaves and needles
   also the remote stars

Far from myself

I imagine a fence crowded

with fugitive parrots

addressing each other sweetly

in english endearments.

From this dry elderly book pages

escape like birds through open windows.

There is zero hope of order

(what have I not made worse).

Clouds slump across hilltops

Steam rises from every brook.

It's mud season again

the redwing blackbirds are back

Yesterday I drove around

listening to the Tale of Genji

on my phone, in my Honda Fit

drinking Dunkin' Donuts coffee.

I had forgotten how he takes up the air,

how even a ghost could decay from

sinister elegance to raucous spite.

Baleful star

I broke all the thin bone china cups also the saucers
I discovered the dry spaciousness of giving up—
        goodbye pleasure
                    hello Ezekiel bread

I wanted not to care and didn't
        my luxury was riddance
                I didn't learn to wait

outside in the flood one of everything bobs past
        farewell to the doomed chair
                    the drowning television
                things look so desirable washing away
                                        sodden paper bouquets

all signs say flee to the mountains   woe to the mortgagees
        say this is the day when everything in your house
                        and then your house—

Pink moon

my grim-reaper-kitten t shirt
   is not in the best of taste

       I don't care
         oh death come purr in my lap
           tonight you can steal my breath

you who ride the bus   who touch the food in the market
who fondle the doorknobs   and shopping cart handles
who go in and out of the houses

like moonlight
like it's your town
it's your town

     like love you
     go anywhere

   sometimes in your long-beaked bird mask
       packed with cloves
         your quaint black robe

         or peering over the doctor's shoulder
           in green scrubs   green mask
             I know you
             how'd you get here so fast

you have so many places to be   sad santa
       the whole earth is yours

    you sit on my chest and grow heavy
      I hold my breath
         keeping it for you

At St. Michael's feet

in the dark museum
taking the form of a little dragon
burnt black, square-headed, crouching
doggish at the angel's feet
the devil is so ugly-cute
you want to take him home
give him a cushion
a little plaid blanket
don't you always make that mistake—
what looked harmless
enters the house
begins to swell and smoke
inhales all the oxygen
for one fiery *whooomp*
and there you are
a charred remnant
in a scorched doorway
and now you can believe
he'd make war in heaven
gnaw the thrones
swat a cherub like a bug

The neighbors hold a work party

chasing invaders: Russian olives
barberry   lesser celandine

& bittersweet: tiny wax flower
                        red clown nose

but I like the starlings and the fireweed
set loose for their prettiness

& wisteria   the way
it'll tear your house down

My solitude

I can just play solitaire on my phone all day
    who's going to save me from that

        it's fine that everything
            is crazy
        still the riddle it always was

it's all alike; we keep on breathing (Keats said that)

        today stemming the tide of boredom
            with a wall of books

        tomorrow—I wonder will you know me
            in my old person suit

scroll down
mr. chicken honks out "Funkytown"
that's not a thing you forget

        some people
        remember their dreams

is it time to leave the house?
I need some things:
    1. spokesperson
    2. less haplessness
    3. (Nevermind
        I'm not going)

bone on bone
one eye peeled

        I traverse the hours like an ant
            crossing a bridge of ants

Stylite

I read the lives
of the stranger saints
and wonder

what made them think god wanted *that?*

a still small voice
     delivers   hints
         like   *hair shirt*
         like   *food is for the weak*
        or   *higher, higher*

in the tradition of extreme
          nothing-doing

standing on this stone pillar
          fully committed

an island of animal stink
          high above arid stones

imagine God
          kissing my mouth

Ex secret policeman

his eye is a black spider
　　　climbing a white curtain
lightless eye of insinuation
on his stool   in a shop   in a college town
　　　　space-cold　　lead-heavy
he resembles a neutron star   one that wants
　　　to take you for questioning
　he waits for his comeback
　　　　the day when he can fully unfold
　　　　　　　can show you who you are

To a billionaire

it's raining diamonds
on Neptune
yes   gems big
as cinder blocks
forever out of reach
of your long long spoon

Late night movie probably about capitalism
(memory from a fifth grade sleepover)

A mysterious factory
appears on a bleak hillside
beyond the town.
A woman walking near it
picks up an odd object.
It bursts & leaves a black mark
on her neck—shiny, a blister, awful.
She sways, she has to lie down.
That night she sleepwalks
to the factory & never
returns. More things happen
while I doze & when I wake
everyone in town is gone
& the hero scientist
is trapped in the factory.
Something dark froths
from a spigot in the locked
white room, his prison.
He yells *They've blocked these pipes*
with human gore! Why have they?
Did I dream this movie? Later,
in a long shot, the factory
explodes, caving in on itself
amid flames.

Secret science

I predict
dizzying revelations

connect the dots
with baroque squiggles

could one be stretched
thin   thin   thin

then snap back
        into a new condition—

now everything
can be repaired

the mirror shows a future
        where I see myself

enjoying a quiet enjoyment
it all makes sense

what a satisfactory day

Dirt is said to heal

Digging, I wait to feel happy—
like *this sunlight is nice*—that moment
when you realize you've felt some gleam of pleasure,
a thing people I know have experienced or so they claim.

Yesterday I picked a blue-black iris. Overnight it died, leaking sad
flower blood the color of mimeo ink
down the side of the white pitcher

Vertigo

between us
so many bridges

over deep rivers over
miscellaneous vacancies

arches rusting
how can I trust

the road to continue
past the bridge's high hump

you know about that girl
on the Mackinac—

how the wind lifted her car
over the rail tipped her

into the lake, so many
weeks spent searching

and there were others
launched into the blue

ask the bridge
for them

close to the edge
a ravenous gravity

wind like a shove
between the shoulders

Empyrean

a silent biplane loops
the loop through blue air
as if up there it's long ago
as if time happened differently
in the sky and looking up
we might see anything—
spaceship or huge shadow
of passenger pigeons
migrating toward absence

Between lives:

It's like standing
caught at the whizzing center
of the world's craziest rotary
trying to cross

Waking you wonder
who am I this time
what damage can I do

Once I was a rat. I gnawed
the foundation of everything

Now you say let life
be one long party
always your day

Later you'll remember
death and all that—
not so much fun
to be king any more

Allegory and fist fight
at every turn a tiger, an ogre, a bandit

This pilgrimage is exhausting.

Who wants to be
the same as yesterday?

Let me just come back as bird, cat, fish,
dragging a little of the past—a fondness
for finery say, so sometimes you see a bright beetle,
a bear in a stolen hat, & guess who

Do you remember?
maybe? kind of. not at all.

At evening

It's not that I don't love the world, say when it's gilded in late light like a movie about Edwardians having a picnic, green hills that swoon into harmless dark, as war comes toward the white dresses—or when shade creeps over the lawn and a cardinal begins his evening chant, a warning to all other cardinals, repeated from his high lair till at some exact degree of dusk he sleeps in the sway.

Acknowledgments

Thanks to the following journals for publishing some of these poems:

Lily Poetry Review "The suffering of suffering" Fall 2024

The Cafe Review "Empyrean", "Bookish House" Spring 2024

Pleiades "My Solitude" 2024

South Florida Poetry Journal "Day" February 2024

Sugar House Review "Summer Twilight" Summer 2023

Tampa Review "The Neighbors Hold a Work Party" Spring 2023,
    "Stylite" Autumn 2024

Bear Review "Condors" May 2023

The Boiler "When to Wear a Tiara" Spring 2023

Bennington Review "As far as this world goes" forthcoming

Cobra Milk "Moon" May 2023

Lily Poetry Review "Disputed Territories" Summer 2022

Quail Bell "cosmographia particularis","Behind You" July 2022

Tipton Poetry Journal "Difficulty" June 2022

QWERTY "Trash Witch", Summer 2022

Radar "Cold Crows" June 2022

About the Author

Martha McCollough is the author of *Wolf Hat Iron Shoes* (Lily Poetry Review Books 2022) and the chapbook *Grandmother Mountain* (Blue Lyra 2019). Her poems have appeared in *Bennington Review, Pleiades, The Boiler, Bear Review,* and *Tampa Review,* among others. Originally from Detroit, she lives in Amherst, MA.

www.ingramcontent.com/pod-product-compliance
Lightning Source LLC
Chambersburg PA
CBHW030515130626
46549CB00007B/3006